30 clearly annotated quotes with context and links.
Perfect for **GCSE** re͏

CW00498468

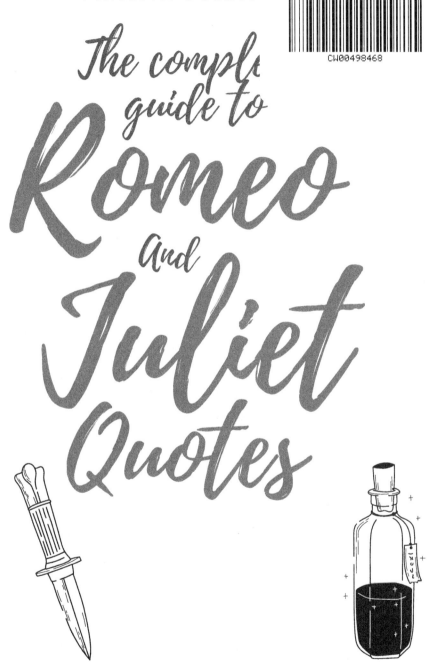

The complet͏
guide to
Romeo
and
Juliet
Quotes

LAURA MCQUIGGIN

The Complete Guide to Romeo and Juliet Quotes by Laura McQuiggin

www.englishtuitiononline.co.uk

First paperback edition September 2022

Cover, and internal design by Laura McQuiggin
Excerpts taken from 'Romeo and Juliet' by William Shakespeare

TABLE OF CONTENTS

Introduction

The Quotes

Practice

Conclusion

FOREWORD

As a tutor, I have taught over 2000 lessons. In those lessons, I have learnt a lot about how students approach their English GCSE examinations and how often students struggle with the Shakespearean text. Most students who find English trickier tend to have more of an affinity for the more 'logical' subjects, like Maths and Science. In response to this, I have devised a system by which a more formulaic approach can be taken to English GCSE questions. The theory behind this guide is that, if you revise the information it contains, you can apply it in a systematic way to an essay and ensure you hit all the assessment objectives. Additionally, there are several blank worksheets to help you to revise your own selection of quotes.

This guide breaks down 30 key quotations from Romeo and Juliet into simple, analytical points, which are easy to understand and build on. Each quotation also has relevant context included and applied to the specific quote. Furthermore, links to relevant moments in the play are included to help develop analysis and provide suggestions as to other points that may be made.

The themes of each quotation are included to enable the guide to be used quickly and easily for practice essays. These themes can also encourage the user to consider the quote from multiple angles - a key part of high-level analysis.

Lastly, each quote contains a short summary of what just happened to add clarity to where the quote has come from. This is especially useful for students who aren't yet confident with the plot.

I hope you find this guide useful - if you do have any questions about the contents, please contact me through my website:
www.englishtuitiononline.co.uk

LAURA MCQUIGGIN

HOW TO USE THIS BOOK

THIS SECTION TELLS YOU WHAT
THEMES AND CHARACTER
QUESTIONS THE QUOTE WILL BEST
RELATE TO.

THIS SECTION GIVES A SUMMARY OF
WHAT HAPPENED BEFORE THE
QUOTATION AND IS USEFUL TO
ENSURE THAT THE QUOTE IS USED
CORRECTLY.

THEMES / CHARACTERS

Lord Capulet
Paris
Juliet
Love
Duty
Family

WHAT JUST HAPPENED

Paris has asked to marry Juliet. Lord Capulet
tries to dissuade him. He says that Juliet is his
only child and so he cannot risk marrying her
off so young. Paris is very insistent and claims
that there are women of Juliet's age who are
already married with children.

Capulet is trying to
persuade Paris to wait

Capulet could be speaking on behalf of his
wife here, further reinforcing gender roles

Makes the waiting appear
picturesque and appealing

Or, he could be trying to
use the royal 'we' to assert
his authority

HERE YOU CAN FIND THE
QUOTATION, THE
TECHNIQUES USED AND A
VARIETY OF POTENTIAL
POINTS OF ANALYSIS
THAT WILL HELP YOU
FUFIL AO2.

Metaphor

Majestic plural

LET TWO MORE SUMMERS WITHER IN THEIR PRIDE, ERE WE MAY THINK HER RIPE TO BE A BRIDE

Rhyming couplet

Comparing her to fruit

Makes it sound
complete and decisive

THE ACT, SCENE NUMBER
AND WHO SAYS THE
QUOTE IS LISTED HERE.

Allows no room for Paris
to argue with Capulet

Demonstrates how Juliet is
perceived as an object

LORD CAPULET - ACT 1 SCENE 2

LINKS

- Lord Capulet initially appears to be a
good father to Juliet. He attempts to
deter Paris's hasty attempts at marriage
due to Juliet's youth.

- Lord Capulet's later decision to allow
Paris to marry Juliet seems unusual given
his initially clear refusal. It could perhaps
suggest that Lord Capulet is a capricious
(changeable) character, or that he was
not genuine in his initial refusal of Paris.

CONTEXT

- In Elizabethan society women were
seen as objects that could be married
off to create alliances. Women were
literally considered to be the property
of their closest male relative, often their
father (or brother if their father was
dead). When a woman was married, she
belonged to her husband. As a result of
this, Lord Capulet is completely in
control of when and to who Juliet gets
married.

16

THIS SECTION WILL HELP YOU
EXPAND YOUR PARAGRAPHS AND
MAKE REFERENCES TO THE PLAY AS
A WHOLE. IT CAN ALSO HELP WITH
DEPTH OF ANALYSIS.

THIS SECTION COVERS A03 AND
PROVIDES EXAMPLES OF RELEVANT
CONTEXTUAL INFORMATION. MAKE
SURE YOU EXPLAIN HOW THIS LINKS
TO THE QUOTATION!

HOW TO REVISE ROMEO AND JULIET

UNDERSTAND THE TEXT

The first thing to do is read the text. Then read it again. Try to read the full text as much as possible before the exam. The more familiar you are with it, the easier it will be to write a top-mark essay! If you aren't keen on reading try listening to an unabridged audiobook: it is just as good!

WATCH ADAPTATIONS

Watching productions of the play is a useful way to recap the key scenes and plot points. It is also useful to see the different ways in which the same scene can be interpreted and portrayed. Try to watch as many different versions as possible and at least one stage production.

MAKE NOTES ON THE KEY PLOT POINTS

Make notes on the key scenes so you have a clear summary of the plot. This will be useful to refer to when you begin writing essays and will be a good resource for revision.

PICK THE BEST QUOTES TO LEARN

This is where 'The Complete Guide to Romeo and Juliet Quotes' comes in! Look through these quotes and pick the ones you feel most confident writing about. It is also worth picking some of your own quotes and preparing them in the same way as is set out in this book. Then start to learn them. It is better to start the learning process as early as possible rather than leaving it to the last minute.

PRACTICE ESSAY QUESTIONS

Practice using the quotes you have learnt to answer essay questions. These can be essays that you have been set at school or ones that you have found online or in this book. Practice makes perfect. It's cliché but it's true! Top tip: if you are short on time, pick an essay question and just practice planning it under timed conditions so you know how you'd structure your essay in the exam.

HOW TO FORMAT QUOTATIONS

SINGLE OR DOUBLE QUOTATION MARKS

You can use either single or double quotation marks. It doesn't matter which. The main thing is that you are consistent. So, whichever you pick, make sure you stick to it!

SHORT OR LONG QUOTES

You don't get marks for the quotes themselves so it's best to stick to shorter quotes. That way you can get straight into the analysis that will get you the marks.

LINE BREAKS

The best practice is to show where the line breaks in the verse are through the / symbol.

(Act 1, Scene 1)
"I hate the word,/As I hate hell, all Montagues, and thee"

SQUARE BRACKETS

When you change something in a quote you should place it in square brackets to demonstrate that a change has been made.

(Act 1, Scene 1)
"saw you him to-day?"

"saw you [Romeo] to-day?"

ELLIPSE

Ellipses can be used to signify information has been removed from a quote. It is a useful way to break longer quotes down into more manageable chunks.

(Act 1, Scene 5)
"He shall be endured:/What, goodman boy! I say, he shall: go to"

"He shall be endured [...] I say, he shall: go to"

THE ASSESSMENT OBJECTIVES

The assessment objectives are the same for GCSE English Literature across all the exam boards. However, the weighting of marks allotted to each objective does vary. Generally, AO1 and AO2 take up the largest part of the mark scheme.

AO1 - WRITING STYLE

Read, understand and respond to texts.
Students should be able to: maintain a critical style and develop an informed personal response, use textual references, including quotations, to support and illustrate interpretations.

AO2 - ANALYSIS

Analyse the language, form and structure used by a writer to create meanings and effects, using relevant subject terminology where appropriate.

AO3 - CONTEXT

Show understanding of the relationships between texts and the contexts in which they were written.

AO4 - SPAG

Use a range of vocabulary and sentence structures for clarity, purpose and effect, with accurate spelling and punctuation.

THE QUOTES

THEMES / CHARACTERS

Romeo
Juliet
Fate
Love
Conflict
Death

SUMMARY

The prologue comes at the start and provides a summary of the plot. It informs the audience that '[t]wo households, both alike in dignity', have been feuding in Verona. It reveals that the children of these families will end the feud with their deaths.

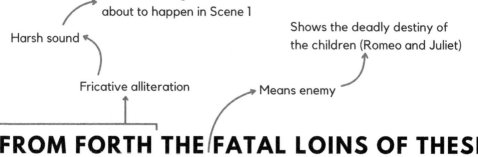

Foreshadowing the violence about to happen in Scene 1

Harsh sound

Fricative alliteration

Shows the deadly destiny of the children (Romeo and Juliet)

Means enemy

FROM FORTH THE FATAL LOINS OF THESE TWO FOES A PAIR OF STAR-CROSS'D LOVERS TAKE THEIR LIFE

Refers to fate

On the one hand, it means they will 'take their life' from Capulet and Montague, e.g. be born from the feuding families

Double meaning

On the other hand, it means they will kill themselves

PROLOGUE

LINKS

- The prologue structurally reinforces the idea that Romeo and Juliet's love is destined to end in tragedy as we are told the outcome before the play even begins. This demonstrates the common belief at the time that your fate was something predestined and unalterable.

- It also sets the tone for the violent start of the play, which is a fight between the Capulet and Montague servants.

CONTEXT

- Shakespeare often took many of the ideas for his plays from other works of literature. 'Romeo and Juliet' is based on 'The Tragicall Historye of Romeus and Juliet', which was written in 1562 by Arthur Brooke. It is a long narrative poem which describes the Capulet and Montague households feuding, and Romeo and Juliet being lovers who are separated by the feud. Both Brooke and Shakespeare start with a 14-line sonnet (here, the prologue), which summarises the plot.

THEMES / CHARACTERS

Tybalt
Benvolio
Conflict
Recklessness
Masculinity
Duty

SUMMARY

Benvolio has just entered to find that the servants of the Capulet and Montague households are having a public fight. Benvolio, being diplomatic in nature, attempts to stop it. Tybalt, a Capulet, enters and challenges him to fight.

Could suggest Tybalt is unable to think beyond violence

Tybalt cannot fathom any reason why Benvolio would have his sword out if he were trying to maintain the peace like he claims

Shows Tybalt's aggression, as it implies he is shouting

Exclamation mark

Means to have his sword out

Juxtaposition

WHAT, DRAWN, AND TALK OF PEACE! I HATE THE WORD, AS I HATE HELL, ALL MONTAGUES, AND THEE

Repetition of 'hate'

Tricolon

Depicts Tybalt as a very angry, aggressive character

His lack of reasoning could suggest there is no real reason for the feud

He doesn't give any reason for his feelings, only states them as absolute fact

TYBALT - ACT 1 SCENE 1

LINKS

- Tybalt's aggressive nature is also shown through his behaviour at Lord Capulet's feast where he demands to fight Romeo.

- Tybalt's desire to fight is further proven when he sends a letter to Romeo summoning him to a duel.

- Benvolio handles the situation well, which demonstrates his peacekeeping nature.

CONTEXT

- In Elizabethan times, fights would be commonplace, and men fighting over their honour was a typical theme both in life and in literature. Tybalt is an exaggerated example of the ideals placed on males at the time. He is fearless and aggressive when it comes to interacting with those he deems his enemies.

SUMMARY

A public brawl has just taken place between the Montagues and the Capulets. Prince Escalus has arrived to restore the peace. He claims this is the third time a fight has broken out and threatens that if it happens again, people will be executed.

He cannot afford to have people continue to go against his orders as it makes him appear weak

Shows the anger that Prince Escalus is feeling

Strong adverb

Reinforcing his power and control

Possessive pronoun

IF EVER YOU DISTURB OUR STREETS AGAIN, YOUR LIVES SHALL PAY THE FORFEIT OF THE PEACE

Foreshadowing

Juxtaposition

Lives are lost to achieve peace between the families

Threatening violence to ensure peace

Ironic

PRINCE ESCALUS - ACT 1 SCENE 1

LINKS

- Prince Escalus's poor leadership can be inferred from his contradictory nature. Here he states that characters will be executed if they are caught fighting again. Yet later, when Romeo is accused of fighting and killing Tybalt, Prince Escalus chooses to have him banished rather than executed.

- The play is structured to begin with violence, with a large fight breaking out in this scene. This demonstrates the severity of the feud.

CONTEXT

- Violence was a common element of Elizabethan society. Entertainment included things such as bear-baiting and hangings. Theatre had to compete with these more violent forms of entertainment and this may explain why 'Romeo and Juliet' has so many moment of brutality in it.

- Prince Escalus's job is to maintain law and order. He would have had the power to hand out punishments and could even have people executed.

THEMES / CHARACTERS

Benvolio
Romeo
Masculinity
Love
Youth

SUMMARY

Romeo has just confessed to Benvolio that he is lovesick. He loves Rosaline and she does not seem to return his affections. Benvolio attempts to cheer Romeo by encouraging him to fall in love with someone else. He says there are lots of beautiful women in Verona.

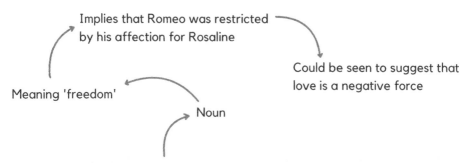

Implies that Romeo was restricted by his affection for Rosaline

Could be seen to suggest that love is a negative force

Meaning 'freedom'

Noun

BY GIVING LIBERTY UNTO THINE EYES; EXAMINE OTHER BEAUTIES

Command

Unusual for Benvolio as he is normally mild-mannered

Reveals that the young men are only looking for beauty as opposed to more substantial love

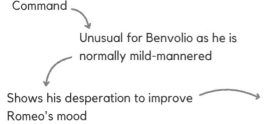

Shows his desperation to improve Romeo's mood

Highlights the fact that he is a good friend to Romeo

BENVOLIO - ACT 1 SCENE 1

LINKS

- Benvolio encourages Romeo to look at other beautiful women in hopes he will fall in love with one of them. Later, Friar Lawrence criticises Romeo for only loving with his eyes and not his heart.

CONTEXT

- While women were expected to be demure, reserved, and abashed at the thought of love and marriage, men had no such limitations placed on them. They were free to openly have feelings for women and to pursue those feelings. They were not limited to only having affection for women they wanted to marry, unlike Juliet who was allowed no such feelings.

THEMES / CHARACTERS

Lord Capulet
Paris
Juliet
Love
Duty
Family

SUMMARY

Paris has asked to marry Juliet. Lord Capulet tries to dissuade him. He says that Juliet is his only child and so he cannot risk marrying her off so young. Paris is very insistent and claims that there are women of Juliet's age who are already married with children.

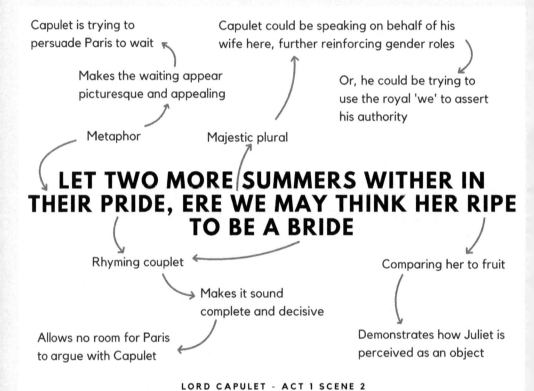

Capulet is trying to persuade Paris to wait

Makes the waiting appear picturesque and appealing

Metaphor

Capulet could be speaking on behalf of his wife here, further reinforcing gender roles

Or, he could be trying to use the royal 'we' to assert his authority

Majestic plural

LET TWO MORE SUMMERS WITHER IN THEIR PRIDE, ERE WE MAY THINK HER RIPE TO BE A BRIDE

Rhyming couplet

Makes it sound complete and decisive

Allows no room for Paris to argue with Capulet

Comparing her to fruit

Demonstrates how Juliet is perceived as an object

LORD CAPULET - ACT 1 SCENE 2

LINKS

- Lord Capulet initially appears to be a good father to Juliet. He attempts to deter Paris's hasty attempts at marriage due to Juliet's youth.

- Lord Capulet's later decision to allow Paris to marry Juliet seems unusual given his initially clear refusal. It could perhaps suggest that Lord Capulet is a capricious (changeable) character, or that he was not genuine in his initial refusal of Paris.

CONTEXT

- In Elizabethan society women were seen as objects that could be married off to create alliances. Women were literally considered to be the property of their closest male relative, often their father (or brother if their father was dead). When a woman was married, she belonged to her husband. As a result of this, Lord Capulet is completely in control of when and to who Juliet gets married.

THEMES / CHARACTERS

Juliet
Lady Capulet
Family
Duty
Youth

SUMMARY

We are introduced to Juliet for the first time. Her mother has called for her and she enters dutifully to ask what her mother would like from her. Juliet's behaviour in the scene continues to be respectful and obedient.

A good example of how a daughter was expected to behave at this time

Shows that Juliet is a dutiful child

Could also imply that Juliet has a more formal/strained relationship with her mother

Respectful address

MADAM, I AM HERE. WHAT IS YOUR WILL?

Suggests that Juliet's relationship with her mother is one sided, where her mother is always expecting things from her, rather than a close personal bond

Question

Juliet seems keen to listen to what her mother has to say

Further showing her loyal nature

JULIET - ACT 1 SCENE 3

LINKS

- Links to Juliet's behaviour during Lord Capulet's feast. She is initially very demure and restrained in her interactions with Romeo. It is only as the conversation progresses and the attraction deepens that she seems to open up and behave more freely.

CONTEXT

- Respect was very important in Shakespeare's time. Children, in particular girls, would have been expected to be obedient and respectful towards their parents.

- Richer families often employed a wet nurse who looked after their children; we see an example of this in Juliet's Nurse. Children who were raised by servants often had very formal relationships with their parents, in stark contrast to what is common today.

THEMES / CHARACTERS

Mercutio
Romeo
Love
Masculinity
Youth
Recklessness

SUMMARY

Romeo has just been explaining his unrequited feelings for Rosaline and how hopeless he feels about love. Mercutio, being a rather brash character, gives him some harsh advice on how to handle the situation.

Reminiscent of the social expectations on men at the time

Makes 'love' seem as though it is actively hurting Romeo

Violent connotations

Draws our attention to the word

Personification

Repetition

IF LOVE BE ROUGH WITH YOU, BE ROUGH WITH LOVE

Contrast

Could suggest that Romeo should become more masculine and get over his lovesickness

Love is typically seen as something precious to be cherished

Or perhaps Mercutio is suggesting Romeo should be more forceful in pursuing Rosaline and not be defeated by her rejection

Mercutio's forceful suggestion implies that he hasn't experienced love himself

MERCUTIO - ACT 1 SCENE 4

LINKS

- This piece of advice tells us a lot about Mercutio's character. It shows him to be brazen and forceful. His personality also becomes relevant when he fights Tybalt in a rash attempt to defend Romeo's honour.

-Mercutio doesn't appear to have any romantic feelings towards any of the characters in the play. This is probably why he is unable to understand Romeo's feelings, and why his tone is so aggressive in this quote.

CONTEXT

- While a lot of attention is often paid to the fact that women had strict standards placed on their behaviours, men were not without expectation. Men, particularly rich men, were expected to be pragmatic, forceful, and robust. Mercutio fits well into these standards, whereas Romeo appears weak. He spends too long moping over his unrequited affections.

THEMES / CHARACTERS

Lord Capulet
Tybalt
Conflict
Masculinity
Duty
Recklessness

SUMMARY

Lord Capulet is having a party at his house. Tybalt has spotted Romeo, a Montague, among the partygoers. He tells Lord Capulet and makes clear his intention to fight Romeo. Lord Capulet insists that Tybalt calm down so he doesn't ruin the party.

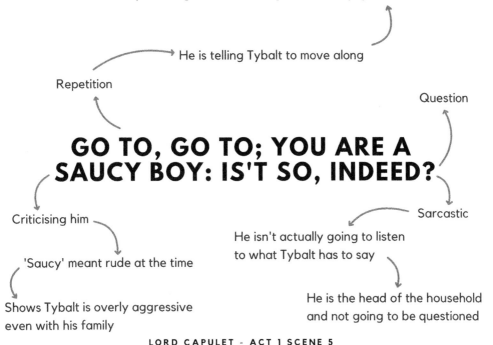

Creates a sense of Capulet's agitation at having his authority questioned

He is telling Tybalt to move along

Repetition

Question

GO TO, GO TO; YOU ARE A SAUCY BOY: IS'T SO, INDEED?

Criticising him

Sarcastic

'Saucy' meant rude at the time

He isn't actually going to listen to what Tybalt has to say

Shows Tybalt is overly aggressive even with his family

He is the head of the household and not going to be questioned

LORD CAPULET - ACT 1 SCENE 5

LINKS

- Shows a more reasonable side to Lord Capulet. Despite the feud, he acknowledges that the feast is not the right time to start a fight.

- Tybalt's decision to continue to push Lord Capulet, despite being told clearly to back down, further shows his unruly behaviour and sets the tone for his duel with Mercutio.

CONTEXT

- Lord Capulet is the head of the household. To have Tybalt refuse to follow his order would have been seen as an insult to Capulet's authority. He shows that he isn't afraid to take charge and orders Tybalt to obey him. This shows that Lord Capulet is a strong male character according to the standards of the time.

THEMES / CHARACTERS

Romeo
Juliet
Love
Religion
Youth
Recklessness

SUMMARY

Romeo and Juliet have just met at Lord Capulet's party. Romeo flirts with Juliet and twists her pious comments into flirtatious remarks. In this quote, he is encouraging her to kiss him by comparing lips to hands coming together in prayer.

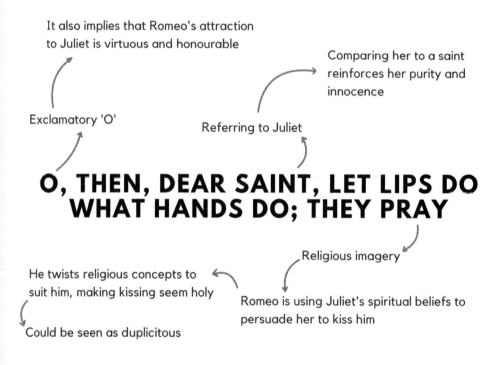

It also implies that Romeo's attraction to Juliet is virtuous and honourable

Exclamatory 'O'

Comparing her to a saint reinforces her purity and innocence

Referring to Juliet

O, THEN, DEAR SAINT, LET LIPS DO WHAT HANDS DO; THEY PRAY

Religious imagery

He twists religious concepts to suit him, making kissing seem holy

Could be seen as duplicitous

Romeo is using Juliet's spiritual beliefs to persuade her to kiss him

ROMEO - ACT 1 SCENE 5

LINKS

- The chaste (modest) nature of the flirtation links with Juliet's character at the beginning of the play. She is meek, obedient and pious.

- Their use of religious imagery could imply a strong faith and this could be seen to explain their faith in, and dependence on, Friar Lawrence for advice later in the play.

CONTEXT

- At the time, the theme of courtly love was a popular one. Courtly love was seen as being polite and restrained. It often included references to religion as seen in this quote.

- Religion was very important at the time. Women were expected to be devout and holy and these were fundamental traits of the ideal Shakespearean women.

THEMES / CHARACTERS

Mercutio
Romeo
Love
Masculinity
Youth

SUMMARY

Romeo has gone missing after Lord Capulet's party. Benvolio and Mercutio are trying to find him in the night time streets of Verona. Benvolio asks Mercutio to call for him.

This suggests that Romeo has been behaving like a 'madman' and 'lover' recently

Mercutio is trying to call his friend using these terms

Listing

Exclamation marks

Demonstrates his recklessness as he does not care about disturbing people

It is night time in Verona

Shows that he is shouting

ROMEO! HUMOURS! MADMAN! PASSION! LOVER! APPEAR THOU IN THE LIKENESS OF A SIGH

Teasing him

Trying to provoke him to retaliate as he would have to show himself to respond

Shows the strong friendship they have

MERCUTIO - ACT 2 SCENE 1

LINKS

Mercutio's description of Romeo in this quote is similar to Lord Montague's description of Romeo when he was in love with Rosaline, who did not return his affections. This could suggest that Romeo often suffers from lovesickness.

The reference to Romeo being a 'madman' links with his later rash and unstable behaviour in the play when he finds out about his banishment and Juliet's death.

CONTEXT

- The freedom that men had meant they could afford to be more open and even playful in their discussion of love and passion. Here, Mercutio makes fun of Romeo by depicting him as a 'madman' due to his intense love (he believes at this point that Romeo still loves Rosaline). It would not have been acceptable for a high-born woman to behave in this way but, because Romeo is a man, it is something that can be joked about.

THEMES / CHARACTERS

Juliet
Romeo
Love
Conflict
Duty
Family

SUMMARY

Juliet is on her balcony. She has just come bac
from Lord Capulet's party where she met
Romeo. She laments the fact that he is a
Capulet and, therefore, an impossible match fc
her. She is unaware that Romeo is standing
below her, listening.

Could highlight her youth or reveal the
depth of love she feels for Romeo

She is frustrated that Romeo is a Montague

Shows her heightened emotion

Shows she understands that the feud will
prevent their marriage

Exclamatory 'O'   Repetition

Rhetorical question:
'Why are you Romeo (Montague)?'

O ROMEO, ROMEO! WHEREFORE ART THOU ROMEO? DENY THY FATHER AND REFUSE THY NAME

Highlights Juliet's innocence
and youth, as she makes it sound
simple for Romeo to leave his family

Commanding tone

Indicates Juliet is more forceful
than she initially appears

JULIET - ACT 2 SCENE 2

LINKS

- Links to Juliet's young age: she does
not understand that she would not be
able to marry Romeo even if he changed
his name and left the Montague family.
It highlights her naivety.

- This quote also reinforces the extent
of the feud, which is so deep that
otherwise suitable matches (in terms of
age, status, and wealth), such as
Romeo, would be disregarded purely
due to the quarrel.

CONTEXT

- Romeo was of a similar social class as
Juliet, so would have been considered
an appropriate match at the time.
However, feuding makes the
relationship impossible. Juliet knows thi
and rather than questioning the feud o
considering being disobedient, she
expresses a childish wish that Romeo
could simply stop being a Montague.

THEMES / CHARACTERS

Juliet
Romeo
Recklessness
Love
Duty
Youth

SUMMARY

Juliet has been speaking from the balcony to Romeo, who is below. They have professed their feelings for one another. Juliet reflects on her own feelings and acknowledges the suddenness of the situation.

Emphasises the amount of concerns that Juliet has about her relationship with Romeo

Suggests that she is unsure of her own judgement

Repetition of 'too'

Juliet would have always had to follow others' orders and thus is unused to independence

IT IS TOO RASH, TOO UNADVISED, TOO SUDDEN

Strong adjectives

Asyndetic listing

Demonstrates that she understands that things are moving too quickly

Increases the pace and gives it a rushed feeling, mimicking the fast paced nature of the relationship

JULIET - ACT 2 SCENE 2

LINKS

- This links to Juliet's initial behaviour as a dutiful and obedient daughter. Her recognition that this love for Romeo might be ill-advised shows her nature is not to rebel. From this, we can infer that it must be true love to make her behave so out of character.

- The caution that she expresses here foreshadows the unhappy events to follow as a result of their 'rash' behaviour.

CONTEXT

- In Shakespearean times, there was a lot of pressure on women, especially young unmarried women, to maintain a flawless reputation. Juliet's realisation that she may be acting too hastily shows her awareness of how the situation could backfire and cause her issues. Romeo, being a young man, would not have had the same pressure, and while running off with a young rich girl would have been very wrong, he would likely have been able to redeem himself socially.

THEMES / CHARACTERS

Friar Lawrence
Romeo
Love
Masculinity
Youth

SUMMARY

Romeo has just confided in Friar Lawrence that he is in love with Juliet. Friar Lawrence is surprised, as he believed Romeo was lovesick over Rosaline. He says 'Is Rosaline, whom thou didst love so dear, [s]o soon forsaken?' He is shocked at how quickly Romeo has moved on.

On the other hand, it could imply that young men's love is false

Often, the focus is on Juliet's age, but Romeo is also young and naive

On the one hand, it could indicate where in the body love is found

Highlights Romeo's youth

Double meaning

YOUNG MEN'S LOVE THEN LIES NOT TRULY IN THEIR HEARTS, BUT IN THEIR EYES

Metaphor

Implies that men only fall in love with women for their appearance

Romeo's love for Juliet sparked suddenly when he knew almost nothing about her, so it must have been based on physical attraction rather than her personality

FRIAR LAWRENCE - ACT 2 SCENE 3

LINKS

- This links to Romeo's initial love for Rosaline. He only loved her for her appearance and quickly moved on to Juliet without thinking of Rosaline again.

- The marriage between Romeo and Juliet happens in such haste they don't actually know much about each other. Therefore we can infer that they 'love' based on appearance rather than personality.

CONTEXT

- Religious leaders were expected to guide their congregants to behave in a holy way and to advise them on religious and personal matters. Here, Friar Lawrence attempts to get Romeo to realise that his 'love' for Rosaline and Juliet is merely lust and not true affection. While socially young men would have been allowed to express desire more than women, lust was still dissuaded in a religious context.

THEMES / CHARACTERS

Juliet
Nurse
Love
Youth
Family

SUMMARY

Juliet is waiting to hear news from Romeo about their marriage. The Nurse has just come back from speaking with Romeo. The Nurse withholds the information she has - teasing Juliet. Juliet becomes increasingly desperate and tries different forms of flattery to get the news out of the Nurse.

Emphasises Juliet's attempt to flatter the Nurse into giving up the information

Hyperbole

Repetition

Tricolon

Reveals Juliet's desperation to find out what Romeo has said

Command

SWEET, SWEET, SWEET NURSE, TELL ME, WHAT SAYS MY LOVE?

Question

Term of endearment

Juliet's desperation to find out information from the Nurse reveals the depth of her desire to marry Romeo

Reinforces Juliet's love for Romeo

JULIET - ACT 2 SCENE 5

LINKS

This links to Juliet's initial behaviour, which is very obedient and sweet. She uses her charms here in an attempt to coax the information from the Nurse. From this, we could infer that she has used her innocent appearance to get her way in the past.

Thus far in the play, the focus has been on Romeo's feelings. This scene shows Juliet's desire to marry Romeo which makes their relationship seem more mutually desirable.

CONTEXT

- Juliet would have been raised from infancy by the Nurse. They have a very strong bond, in contrast to the formal relationship Juliet has with her mother. This is shown by the Nurse's teasing behaviour in this scene.

- The Nurse represents the working class, who would also be in the original audience. The Nurse is a stereotype of the lower classes and this is shown through her often inappropriate behaviour and jokes.

Friar Lawrence
Romeo
Juliet
Love
Fate
Death

SUMMARY

Friar Lawrence has agreed to marry Romeo to Juliet. Romeo and the Friar are waiting in the cell for Juliet to arrive so that the marriage can take place. Friar Lawrence is shown to be cautious and tries to warn Romeo to be more moderate in his affection for Juliet.

Which could be Friar Lawrence criticising the hasty marriage

An older meaning of the word violent is 'doing something quickly'

Draws attention to the word and mirrors the frequency of violence in Verona

Repetition of 'violent'

Juxtaposition

THESE VIOLENT DELIGHTS HAVE VIOLENT ENDS

Foreshadows the end of the play

'End' can also be a euphemism for death

Further reinforces the idea that they are fated to die

FRIAR LAWRENCE - ACT 2 SCENE 6

LINKS

- This clearly links with the violent ending of the play when Paris is murdered and Romeo and Juliet both commit suicide.

- It also shows that Friar Lawrence is very knowledgeable. He is presented as the voice of reason, as he accurately predicts that their strong affection will have harsh consequences. However, his advice is ignored.

CONTEXT

- Friar Lawrence would have been seen as a wise individual, whose position as religious leader made him uniquely well placed to give advice on matters of importance. His warning here is proven correct later in the play, which further supports the idea that he is an intelligent guide.

THEMES / CHARACTERS

Mercutio
Romeo
Tybalt
Duty
Conflict
Masculinity

SUMMARY

Tybalt has challenged Romeo to a fight. Romeo, newly married to Juliet, does not want to fight Tybalt as he is related to Juliet. Romeo refuses to fight and says he cannot explain why. Mercutio takes this to be a sign of weakness and fights Tybalt on Romeo's behalf.

Demonstrates his anger at the situation

Emphasises how Romeo's behaviour is against what was expected of him at the time: even his friends are angry with him

Exclamatory 'O'

Asyndetic listing

O CALM, DISHONOURABLE, VILE SUBMISSION!

Exclamation mark

Because of this, 'submission' was often associated with feminine behaviour

Wives were supposed to be submissive to their husbands

Mercutio could be attempting to embarrass Romeo and provoke him into fighting

Suggests he is shouting, demonstrating his recklessness and foreshadowing the fight that follows

MERCUTIO - ACT 3 SCENE 1

LINKS

- Romeo's behaviour throughout the play thus far has been traditionally feminine. This is seen particularly in the opening scene when Romeo is said to have been weeping over his unrequited love, Rosaline.

- Mercutio's character is presented as reckless. His rash decision to step into the fight can be foreshadowed by his earlier risky behaviour, such as sneaking into Capulet's party and the advice he gives Romeo.

CONTEXT

- There were strong ideas around honour, and it was expected that a man would fight to protect his honour. As Romeo refused to fight Tybalt, it would seem as though he had no honour, courage, or sense of duty. Mercutio's decision to step in for Romeo is an attempt to save his friend's reputation and, by extent, his own.

THEMES / CHARACTERS

Mercutio
Romeo
Death
Conflict
Masculinity
Friendship

SUMMARY

Mercutio has decided to fight Tybalt because Romeo refused to. Romeo tries to intervene and end the fight, which results in Mercutio being stabbed. Mercutio, dying from his wounds, curses both the Capulet and the Montague families.

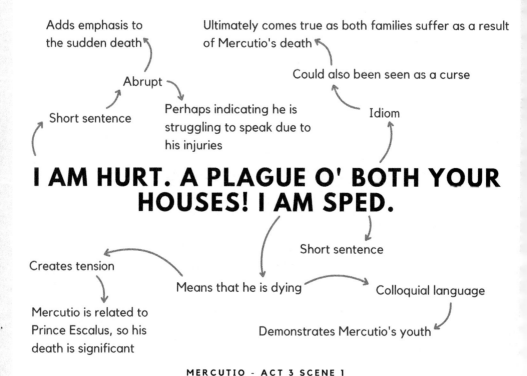

Adds emphasis to the sudden death

Ultimately comes true as both families suffer as a result of Mercutio's death

Abrupt

Could also been seen as a curse

Short sentence

Perhaps indicating he is struggling to speak due to his injuries

Idiom

I AM HURT. A PLAGUE O' BOTH YOUR HOUSES! I AM SPED.

Creates tension

Short sentence

Means that he is dying

Colloquial language

Mercutio is related to Prince Escalus, so his death is significant

Demonstrates Mercutio's youth

MERCUTIO - ACT 3 SCENE 1

LINKS

- Mercutio is related to Prince Escalus and so is technically impartial in the feud. However, his association with Romeo and Benvolio implies that he sides with the Capulets. Here it is clear that he feels anger towards both sides now that he has been mortally injured.

- Later, it is a plague that prevents Romeo from receiving the message about Juliet's fake death. So, ultimately, a plague does cause death for both houses.

CONTEXT

- The Globe could originally hold around 3000 people, so was very busy and noisy at points. The phrase 'to hear a play' was used, rather than 'to see a play'. The majority of the audience were 'groundlings' who stood around the stage. Shakespeare often had his characters announce their actions to help those without a clear view of the stage understand what was going on. This is why Mercutio loudly announces that '[he] is hurt' and '[he] is sped' (dead).

THEMES / CHARACTERS

Romeo
Juliet
Masculinity
Conflict
Duty

SUMMARY

Tybalt just mortally injured Mercutio. Romeo feels guilty because Mercutio was fighting on his behalf. Romeo had refused to fight Tybalt himself because Tybalt was related to Juliet. He now blames Juliet for his 'weakness'.

Demonstrates his genuine love for Juliet as he uses endearing language to refer to her, even when speaking an aside (to himself)

Exclamatory 'O'

Term of endearment

Rather than taking responsibility for his actions, Romeo seeks to move the blame to Juliet

O SWEET JULIET, THY BEAUTY HATH MADE ME EFFEMINATE

Strong verb

Implies that she has forced him to become this way

Indicates that being with Juliet has caused him to become gentler and weaker

Making him less of a man

ROMEO - ACT 3 SCENE 1

LINKS

Romeo's attitude at the beginning of the play could also be considered 'effeminate' as he is constantly depicted weeping over Rosaline.

His emotions continue to control him throughout the remainder of the play and lead to his suicide.

CONTEXT

- The strict binary gender roles of the time meant that any behaviour that was considered weak would have been considered feminine. Romeo's refusal to fight would have been seen as a weakness that emasculated him.

THEMES / CHARACTERS

Lady Capulet
Romeo
Prince Escalus
Family
Love
Conflict

SUMMARY

Romeo just killed Tybalt as revenge for Mercutio's murder. Benvolio explains what happened. Lady Capulet, who is Tybalt's relative, claims that Benvolio is lying to protect Romeo when he says that Tybalt killed Mercutio.

This demonstrates the perceived strength of family ties: Benvolio's blood connection to Romeo is what convinces Lady Capulet that he would lie to protect Romeo, rather than the fact that they are good friends.

Meaning family or a relation

Refers to the Montagues as a collective

HE IS A KINSMAN TO THE MONTAGUE; AFFECTION MAKES HIM FALSE; HE SPEAKS NOT TRUE

Hypocritical

Repetition

Her affection for Tybalt is what is causing her to blame Romeo

This shows how forceful she is being

Paints a rather negative picture of Lady Capulet

She wants revenge for Tybalt's death

LADY CAPULET - ACT 3 SCENE 1

LINKS

- In an attempt to get justice for Tybalt, Lady Capulet displays more concern here than she does when Juliet desperately pleads with her parents to stop her marriage to Paris. Then she says 'I would the fool [meaning Juliet] were married to her grave!' Her lack of sympathy for her daughter contrasts with her clear affection for Tybalt.

CONTEXT

- Loyalty and duty were very important traits in Shakespearean times. Relative were expected to support each other. Lady Capulet uses this societal expectation to refute Benvolio's explanation of what happened, implyin that he is lying to protect Romeo, to whom he is related.

THEMES / CHARACTERS

Juliet
Nurse
Romeo
Duty
Love

SUMMARY

The Nurse just told Juliet that Tybalt has been killed in a fight and Romeo is the killer. She speaks badly of Romeo and weeps for Tybalt. Juliet criticises the Nurse, saying that her loyalty is now to her husband, Romeo, and the Nurse should not speak badly of him.

This shows despite her loyalty the marriage must be kept secret

Juliet refuses to speak against her husband

Perhaps concerned she will be overheard

Pronoun

'Ill' means badly

Avoids naming him

SHALL I SPEAK ILL OF HIM THAT IS MY HUSBAND?

Despite the recent nature of the marriage and Juliet's young age, she recognises her role as a wife is to support her husband

Question

Could be interpreted as sarcastic

Juliet is daring the Nurse to tell her otherwise

JULIET - ACT 3 SCENE 2

LINKS

- Juliet is shown to be a dutiful and obedient young woman of her time. Her only fault is her love for Romeo and her rash marriage to him. Here, she reverts to more traditional behaviour.

- She is also reprimanding the Nurse in this scene, criticising her for her treatment of Romeo. This shows that despite the Nurse being older and having raised Juliet, she is still a servant, and Juliet is still her mistress and can chastise her.

CONTEXT

- Women were seen as the property of their closest male relatives. As Juliet is now married, she belongs to Romeo and is expected to be dutiful and obedient to him. After her initial shock at Tybalt's murder, she realises that she had not been speaking about Romeo in the respectful manner that befits a good wife.

THEMES / CHARACTERS

Romeo
Juliet
Love
Death
Recklessness

SUMMARY

Romeo has been hiding, waiting to hear his punishment for killing Tybalt. Friar Lawrence arrives to tell him that, rather than have Romeo executed, Prince Escalus has banished him from Verona, which is a lesser sentence. Romeo is upset as he won't be able to see Juliet.

For him, it is not better as it means that he will not be able to spend time with Juliet

Presents Romeo's contempt for the lesser sentence

Shows Romeo's heightened emotion in this scene

Derisive laugh

Exclamation mark

HA, BANISHMENT! BE MERCIFUL, SAY 'DEATH'

Juxtaposition

Would rather be sentenced to 'death'

Perhaps Romeo is so caught up in his emotions that he is unable to think rationally and accept that 'banishment' is a lesser punishment than 'death'

Alludes to the death of both Romeo and Juliet at the end of the play

ROMEO - ACT 3 SCENE 3

LINKS

- This links to the description of Romeo at the beginning, where he appears to be so lovesick over Rosaline that he has lost the ability to assess the situation rationally and feels that life is hopeless.

- This also reinforces the strong love that Romeo has for Juliet, as he would prefer to be executed to being banished and prevented from seeing her.

CONTEXT

- Christianity was the main religion in Shakespearean times. The majority of the population saw Heaven and Hell as very real places. Romeo's reaction here seems more logical because of this contextual information, as he believes that death would result in him going to Heaven. For him, this would be better than being banished and parted from his beloved Juliet.

THEMES / CHARACTERS

Lord Capulet
Paris
Love
Duty
Authority
Family

SUMMARY

Friar Lawrence has encouraged Romeo to consummate his marriage with Juliet and then leave Verona until the marriage can be made public and Romeo's banishment is revoked. Lord Capulet, unaware of this, speaks to Paris and agrees to let him marry Juliet.

He has high status and is related to the Prince so would have been a very eligible bachelor

Highlights Paris's position in society

Respectful address

Suggests that Capulet is keen to find a way to console Juliet and implies that he does genuinely care for her

Powerful adjective

SIR PARIS, I WILL MAKE A DESPERATE TENDER OF MY CHILD'S LOVE: I THINK SHE WILL BE RULED IN ALL RESPECTS BY ME; NAY, MORE, I DOUBT IT NOT

Brings to mind connotations of royalty/ruling: in this case, Capulet is the king and Juliet is his subject

Further demonstrates the power structures in a patriarchal society

Strong statement

Proves Juliet has been a loyal daughter in the past as Capulet has no reason to doubt that she will obey him

LORD CAPULET - ACT 3 SCENE 4

LINKS

This links to Lord Capulet's initial refusal of Paris's petition to marry Juliet. It could perhaps suggest that Capulet is indecisive and changeable.

It could also be interpreted as a genuine attempt to help his daughter recover from her apparent grief over the death of Tybalt. Lady Capulet cites this as a reason for the marriage when she explains the plan to Juliet.

CONTEXT

- Marriage was a way for the rich to create connections with other rich families. Paris would have been considered a very good match for Juliet as he is related to Prince Escalus.

- Lord Capulet does not know about Juliet's marriage to Romeo and so believes that Juliet is still obedient to him and as such does not anticipate her refusal. He does not even bother to ask her in advance how she would feel about marrying Paris.

THEMES / CHARACTERS

Juliet
Romeo
Fate
Love
Death

SUMMARY

Romeo and Juliet have just spent their wedding night together. Romeo needs to leave before dawn so he can flee the city without being caught. They say regretful goodbyes to each other as he descends from the balcony.

Perhaps Juliet is subconsciously aware that their relationship cannot work

Shows that Juliet is shocked by what she thinks she sees

Exclamatory 'O'

Exclamation mark

O GOD, I HAVE AN ILL-DIVINING SOUL! METHINKS I SEE THEE, NOW THOU ART BELOW, AS ONE DEAD IN THE BOTTOM O A TOMB

Prophetic image

Foreshadowing

The melancholic tone reinforces the tragic nature of Romeo and Juliet's love

Later in the play, Juliet wakes to find Romeo dead in the tomb

JULIET - ACT 3 SCENE 5

LINKS

- Juliet's fascination with death is also explored in her soliloquy before she takes the potion that Friar Lawrence gave her. In her speech, she worries about waking up alone in the tomb, going mad and playing with the bones of her relatives. "O, if I wake, shall I not be distraught,/Environed with all these hideous fears?/And madly play with my forefather's joints?"

CONTEXT

- The idea of destiny, where you had a set path in life and were unable to change it, was common and fascinated the Shakespearean audience. Here Juliet foresees their tragic destiny. The audience were told the protagonists wi die in the prologue. They would have understood Romeo and Juliet's fate wa predestined and thus inescapable, creating sympathy for the young couple.

THEMES / CHARACTERS

Lord Capulet
Lady Capulet
Juliet
Family
Authority
Duty

SUMMARY

Lady Capulet told Juliet that she must marry Paris. Juliet refused. Lord Capulet enters to find out why. He is shocked at Juliet's disobedience and threatens to hit her ('my fingers itch') and disown her if she refuses to marry Paris.

Perhaps his emotions are preventing him from judging and handling the situation in a more suitable manner

Suggests he is not thinking clearly

Highlights the strength of emotion Lord Capulet feels and reveals his aggressive nature

Increases the pace

Short sentences

Highlights her youth

Exclamation mark suggests he is shouting

HANG THEE, YOUNG BAGGAGE! DISOBEDIENT WRETCH!

Shows that his anger stems from Juliet's decision to go against what he wants her to do

Insult

In this context, it means 'a despicable person'

His authority, and thus his masculinity, is being questioned by her disobedience

LORD CAPULET - ACT 3 SCENE 5

LINKS

- This is a huge contrast to Lord Capulet at the beginning of the play. Before, he seemed to be a reasonable and considerate father, especially by the standards of the time.

- Here he is attempting to assert his authority over his daughter. This is similar to his efforts to control Tybalt during the feast.

CONTEXT

- Marriage was seen as the main goal for women. All women were expected to either get married or devote their lives to God by joining a nunnery. Juliet's refusal would have shocked Lord Capulet because her function as a daughter was to marry well and create a connection with another wealthy family. Paris would have been considered a very eligible bachelor.

THEMES / CHARACTERS

Paris
Juliet
Love
Masculinity
Duty
Religion

SUMMARY

After refusing to marry Paris, Juliet goes to Friar Lawrence to ask for his advice. She meets Paris on the way. Paris tries to flirt with her. He says that she must not be embarrassed to tell the Friar of the love she has for him when she makes her confession.

Might suggest that Paris genuinely believes that Juliet cares for him

Friar Lawrence is holding confession and Paris believes that Juliet is going to the Friar to confess her 'sinful' feelings for him

Commanding tone

Meaning Friar Lawrence

DO NOT DENY TO HIM THAT YOU LOVE ME

The forcefulness could suggest that Paris is afraid that Juliet does not love him

He has wanted to marry her for a long time

Another interpretation is that he is being forceful in an attempt to reassure himself that Juliet must care for him

PARIS - ACT 4 SCENE 1

LINKS

- Capulet initially told Paris to try and 'woo' Juliet. While we don't ever see Paris and Juliet interact in the play, it is possible that they have spoken and Paris may have attempted to follow Lord Capulet's advice. This might explain why he is so forthright with her, as he believes her to genuinely be in love with him.

CONTEXT

- As women were expected to be obedient and submissive, is likely that Paris believed that Juliet would love him as her future husband. Women were also expected to be demure and innocent, so Paris could have been interpreting her cold behaviour as an attempt to conceal her true affection for him. This would have been seen as a mark of a pure, pious woman, who was rightfully abashed at feeling romantic notions towards a man - even if they were to be married.

THEMES / CHARACTERS

Juliet
Friar Lawrence
Love
Religion
Death

SUMMARY

Friar Lawrence came up with a plan. He gave Juliet a potion to make her look like she was dead so she could get out of the marriage. Now, she is alone in her room about to take the potion. She worries as to what might happen.

Shows Juliet's panic and inability to think clearly

Reinforces her panic as she is starting to suspect someone whom she has trusted and relied on

Starting to become suspicious of the Friar

Long sentence

WHAT IF IT BE A POISON, WHICH THE FRIAR SUBTLY HATH MINISTER'D TO HAVE ME DEAD, LEST IN THIS MARRIAGE HE SHOULD BE DISHONOUR'D

Blunt language

Reveals Juliet's realisation of what is at stake

Reveals the consequence for Friar Lawrence if he ends up marrying Juliet to Paris when he has already married her to Romeo

JULIET - ACT 4 SCENE 3

LINKS

While the Friar told Juliet to agree to marry Paris, he could not actually allow them to wed, as she was already married and that would be bigamy. This was legal and seen as sinful. It would have tarnished the Friar's reputation, and so Juliet wonders whether he plans to simply poison her so he does not have to deal with the consequences of marrying her to Paris.

CONTEXT

- Anti-Catholic sentiment was high in England at this time. This could mean that the audience might be suspicious of the Catholic Friar and his motives. Although he appears well-meaning, most of his advice ends in disaster and death.

- Catholicism does not permit bigamy and so Friar Lawrence would also be committing a sin if he allowed Paris to marry Juliet.

THEMES / CHARACTERS

Nurse
Juliet
Love
Family
Duty
Death

SUMMARY

The Nurse just arrived to wake Juliet up for the wedding. She finds Juliet dead and calls for help. Lord and Lady Capulet enter and are shocked. They all mourn over Juliet's body, in disbelief at her sudden death.

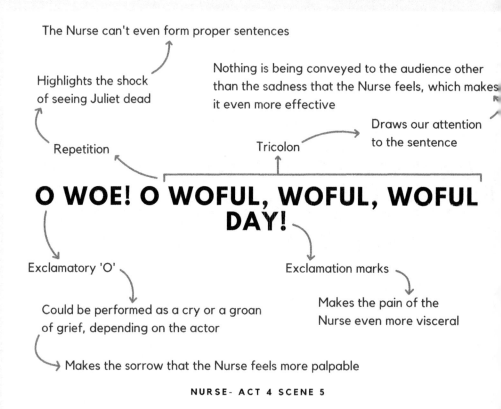

The Nurse can't even form proper sentences

Highlights the shock of seeing Juliet dead

Nothing is being conveyed to the audience other than the sadness that the Nurse feels, which makes it even more effective

Draws our attention to the sentence

Repetition

Tricolon

O WOE! O WOFUL, WOFUL, WOFUL DAY!

Exclamatory 'O'

Could be performed as a cry or a groan of grief, depending on the actor

Makes the sorrow that the Nurse feels more palpable

Exclamation marks

Makes the pain of the Nurse even more visceral

NURSE- ACT 4 SCENE 5

LINKS

- Throughout the play, it is clear that Juliet and the Nurse have a very strong bond.

- The Nurse often goes against what she ought to be doing to support Juliet's relationship with Romeo. This shows that she genuinely cares about Juliet's feelings, whereas Juliet's mother is not affected by her daughter's reluctance to marry Paris, suggesting a more strained connection.

CONTEXT

- As the Nurse would have been far more involved in raising Juliet than Lady Capulet, it is logical that she would genuinely grieve over her mistress's death. Juliet was like a daughter to the Nurse and they had a strong bond, which explains this reaction.

- The Nurse might also be concerned that Juliet's death could be seen as her failure to look after Juliet. The Nurse normally slept in Juliet's room, so this night was an exception.

THEMES / CHARACTERS

Romeo
Fate
Love
Death
Recklessness

SUMMARY

Romeo has just heard of Juliet's sudden death. He does not know that she is actually alive. He expresses his anger at fate for keeping them apart and plans to kill himself to be reunited with her.

Romeo is finally acting according to the standards of the time by being forceful and authoritative

The stars symbolised fate, which reiterates the idea that the relationship is predestined to end in tragedy

Makes the stars seem to actively conspire against Romeo

Romeo is talking to the stars as though they are human

Commanding tone

Direct address

Personification

THEN I DEFY YOU, STARS!

Short sentence

Exclamation mark

Draws attention to the forceful remark

Shows the passion and anger that Romeo feels

Could suggest Romeo's determination

ROMEO - ACT 5 SCENE 1

LINKS

- This links to the 'star-crossed' nature of Romeo and Juliet's relationship, which is stated in the prologue.

- Romeo quickly decides that he must kill himself so he can be reunited with Juliet. He previously mentioned killing himself when he was first told of his banishment, suggesting that he is unable to handle the strong emotions that he feels.

CONTEXT

- In Shakespearean times, people believed that certain things in life, like status and death, were predestined and thus unalterable. Despite the young couple's attempts to make their relationship work, it is fated to end in tragedy. Here Romeo is trying to go against fate by deciding to kill himself, thus re-joining Juliet in death.

THEMES / CHARACTERS

Juliet
Love
Fate
Death
Recklessness

SUMMARY

Juliet has just awoken in the tomb to find that Romeo, believing she was dead, has killed himself. Juliet refuses to leave with the Friar and instead stabs herself so that she can be with Romeo again.

For Juliet, death is a 'happy' alternative to life without Romeo

Shows the tragedy of the situation

The human emotion of happiness juxtaposes with the sadness of the scene

Reveals the heightened emotion of the line

Exclamatory 'O'

Personification

Exclamation mark

O HAPPY DAGGER! THIS IS THY SHEATH; THERE RUST, AND LET ME DIE

Metaphor

The use of 'let' suggests that death is something that Juliet really wants

Implying that the proper place for the dagger is in her, again supporting ideas of fate and destiny

JULIET - ACT 5 SCENE 3

LINKS

- This links to the love that Juliet is shown to have for Romeo throughout the play. Her love is genuine and strong, which is why she is willing to kill herself to join him.

- An alternative interpretation is that this reasserts Juliet's youth and naivety. No emotionally mature person would act in the way she does, which suggests she is too young to handle the intense relationship.

CONTEXT

- Suicide was considered to be a sin and was also illegal in Shakespeare's time. Those who committed suicide could not be buried in holy ground. The public condemnation of suicide also led to a certain fascination with it. Suicide occurs in many of Shakespeare's plays. Characters who commit suicide include Lady Macbeth, Ophelia, Goneril, Othello, and Cleopatra.

THEMES / CHARACTERS

Lord Capulet
Lord Montague
Death
Friendship
Conflict
Fate

SUMMARY

The Capulets and the Montagues have just arrived to find Romeo and Juliet dead. They grieve over their children and decide to end the feud, as it has taken too many lives.

Shows the grief that Capulet feels over the death of his daughter, Juliet

Juxtaposes with previous relationship as 'enemies'

Implies a close familial connection

Exclamatory 'O'

Term of endearment

O BROTHER MONTAGUE, GIVE ME THY HAND: THIS IS MY DAUGHTER'S OINTURE, FOR NO MORE CAN I DEMAND

Offering to shake his hand

A sign of respect

Rhyme

Gives the couplet a sense of completion

This adds finality to the ending of the feud and the death of Romeo and Juliet

LORD CAPULET - ACT 5 SCENE 3

LINKS

Contrast to the beginning of the play where Lord Montague and Lord Capulet were calling for their swords to fight each other. Now Capulet calls him 'brother'.

This proves that the warning from the prologue 'doth with their death bury their parents' strife' was true. Romeo's and Juliet's deaths put an end to the feud.

CONTEXT

- A 'jointure' was a sum of money to be paid to a widow in the event of her husband's death. It was intended to help the widow maintain her lifestyle and could act as a dowry in the event of remarriage. In this case, Capulet asks for a handshake instead of money as 'jointure'. He admits that he can ask for no more from Montague.

BLANK QUOTE WORKSHEETS

THEMES / CHARACTERS

SUMMARY

66

99

SAID BY

LINKS

CONTEXT

66

99

SAID BY

THEMES / CHARACTERS

SUMMARY

" "

LINKS

CONTEXT

THEMES / CHARACTERS

SUMMARY

66

99

LINKS

CONTEXT

THEMES / CHARACTERS

SUMMARY

66

99

SAID BY

LINKS

CONTEXT

THEMES / CHARACTERS

SUMMARY

" "

_____

LINKS

CONTEXT

THEMES / CHARACTERS

SUMMARY

“

”

LINKS

CONTEXT

49

THEMES / CHARACTERS

SUMMARY

“

”

SAID BY

LINKS

CONTEXT

THEMES / CHARACTERS

SUMMARY

"

"

LINKS

CONTEXT

THEMES / CHARACTERS

SUMMARY

66

99

SAID BY

LINKS

CONTEXT

THEMES / CHARACTERS

SUMMARY

"

"

SAID BY

LINKS

CONTEXT

THEMES / CHARACTERS

SUMMARY

66

99

SAID BY

LINKS

CONTEXT

66

99

SAID BY

LINKS

CONTEXT

THEMES / CHARACTERS

SUMMARY

66

99

LINKS

CONTEXT

THEMES / CHARACTERS

SUMMARY

" "

LINKS

CONTEXT

THEMES / CHARACTERS

SUMMARY

"

"

LINKS

CONTEXT

THEMES / CHARACTERS

SUMMARY

66

99

SAID BY

LINKS

CONTEXT

THEMES / CHARACTERS

SUMMARY

66

99

SAID BY

LINKS

CONTEXT

THEMES / CHARACTERS

SUMMARY

66

99

LINKS

CONTEXT

THEMES / CHARACTERS

SUMMARY

66

99

SAID BY

LINKS

CONTEXT

PRACTICE QUESTIONS

QUESTION 1

Read the following extract from Act 1 Scene 1 of *Romeo and Juliet* and then answer the question that follows.

At this point in the play, the Capulets and Montagues have been fighting in the street.

PRINCE:
Rebellious subjects, enemies to peace,
Profaners of this neighbour-stained steel,--
Will they not hear? What, ho! you men, you beasts,
That quench the fire of your pernicious rage
With purple fountains issuing from your veins,
On pain of torture, from those bloody hands
Throw your mistemper'd weapons to the ground,
And hear the sentence of your moved prince.
Three civil brawls, bred of an airy word,
By thee, old Capulet, and Montague,
Have thrice disturb'd the quiet of our streets,
And made Verona's ancient citizens
Cast by their grave beseeming ornaments,
To wield old partisans, in hands as old,
Canker'd with peace, to part your canker'd hate:
If ever you disturb our streets again,
Your lives shall pay the forfeit of the peace.
For this time, all the rest depart away:
You Capulet; shall go along with me:
And, Montague, come you this afternoon,
To know our further pleasure in this case,
To old Free-town, our common judgment-place.
Once more, on pain of death, all men depart.

Exeunt all but MONTAGUE, LADY MONTAGUE, and
BENVOLIO

Starting with this speech, explore how Shakespeare presents the theme of rivalry.

Write about:
- how Shakespeare presents rivalry in this extract
- how Shakespeare presents the theme of rivalry in the play as a whole

[30 marks]
AO4 [4 marks]

THE PLAN

PARAGRAPH 1:

PARAGRAPH 2:

PARAGRAPH 3:

QUESTION 2

Read the following extract from Act 1 Scene 2 of *Romeo and Juliet* and then answer the question that follows.

At this point in the play, Paris has just asked if he can marry Lord Capulet's daughter, Juliet.

CAPULET:
But saying o'er what I have said before:
My child is yet a stranger in the world;
She hath not seen the change of fourteen years,
Let two more summers wither in their pride,
Ere we may think her ripe to be a bride.
PARIS:
Younger than she are happy mothers made.
CAPULET:
And too soon marr'd are those so early made.
The earth hath swallow'd all my hopes but she,
She is the hopeful lady of my earth:
But woo her, gentle Paris, get her heart,
My will to her consent is but a part;
An she agree, within her scope of choice
Lies my consent and fair according voice.
This night I hold an old accustom'd feast,
Whereto I have invited many a guest,
Such as I love; and you, among the store,
One more, most welcome, makes my number more.
At my poor house look to behold this night
Earth-treading stars that make dark heaven light:
Such comfort as do lusty young men feel
When well-apparell'd April on the heel
Of limping winter treads, even such delight
Among fresh female buds shall you this night
Inherit at my house; hear all, all see,
And like her most whose merit most shall be:
Which on more view, of many mine being one
May stand in number, though in reckoning none,
Come, go with me.

Starting with this speech, explore how far Shakespeare presents Lord Capulet as a good father.

Write about:
* how Shakespeare presents Lord Capulet in this extract
* how far Shakespeare presents Lord Capulet as a good father in the play as a whole

[30 marks]
AO4 [4 marks]

THE PLAN

PARAGRAPH 1:

PARAGRAPH 2:

PARAGRAPH 3:

QUESTION 3

Read the following extract from Act 1 Scene 5 of *Romeo and Juliet* and then answer the question that follows.

At this point in the play, Tybalt has spotted Romeo, a Montague, at Capulet's feast.

TYBALT:
Uncle, this is a Montague, our foe,
A villain that is hither come in spite,
To scorn at our solemnity this night.
CAPULET:
Young Romeo is it?
TYBALT:
'Tis he, that villain Romeo.
CAPULET:
Content thee, gentle coz, let him alone;
He bears him like a portly gentleman;
And, to say truth, Verona brags of him
To be a virtuous and well-govern'd youth:
I would not for the wealth of all the town
Here in my house do him disparagement:
Therefore be patient, take no note of him:
It is my will, the which if thou respect,
Show a fair presence and put off these frowns,
And ill-beseeming semblance for a feast.
TYBALT:
It fits, when such a villain is a guest:
I'll not endure him.
CAPULET:
He shall be endured:
What, goodman boy! I say, he shall: go to;
Am I the master here, or you? go to.
You'll not endure him! God shall mend my soul!
You'll make a mutiny among my guests!
You will set cock-a-hoop! you'll be the man!
TYBALT:
Why, uncle, 'tis a shame.

Starting with this speech, explore how Shakespeare presents the character of Tybalt.

Write about:
- how Shakespeare presents Tybalt in this extract
- how Shakespeare presents Tybalt in the play as a whole

[30 marks]
AO4 [4 marks]

THE PLAN

PARAGRAPH 1:

PARAGRAPH 2:

PARAGRAPH 3:

QUESTION 4

Read the following extract from Act 2 Scene 2 of *Romeo and Juliet* and then answer the question that follows.

At this point in the play, Romeo is standing below Juliet's balcony. Juliet does not know that he is there.

> **ROMEO:**
> He jests at scars that never felt a wound.
>
> *JULIET appears above at a window*
>
> But, soft! what light through yonder window breaks?
> It is the east, and Juliet is the sun.
> Arise, fair sun, and kill the envious moon,
> Who is already sick and pale with grief,
> That thou her maid art far more fair than she:
> Be not her maid, since she is envious;
> Her vestal livery is but sick and green
> And none but fools do wear it; cast it off.
> It is my lady, O, it is my love!
> O, that she knew she were!
> She speaks yet she says nothing: what of that?
> Her eye discourses; I will answer it.
> I am too bold, 'tis not to me she speaks:
> Two of the fairest stars in all the heaven,
> Having some business, do entreat her eyes
> To twinkle in their spheres till they return.
> What if her eyes were there, they in her head?
> The brightness of her cheek would shame those stars,
> As daylight doth a lamp; her eyes in heaven
> Would through the airy region stream so bright
> That birds would sing and think it were not night.
> See, how she leans her cheek upon her hand!
> O, that I were a glove upon that hand,
> That I might touch that cheek!

Starting with this speech, explore how Shakespeare presents the theme of desire.

Write about:
- how Shakespeare presents desire in this extract
- how Shakespeare presents the theme of desire in the play as a whole

[30 marks]
AO4 [4 marks]

THE PLAN

PARAGRAPH 1:

PARAGRAPH 2:

PARAGRAPH 3:

QUESTION 5

Read the following extract from Act 5 Scene 3 of *Romeo and Juliet* and then answer the question that follows.

At this point in the play, Romeo and Juliet have been found dead in the tomb. Friar Lawrence has explained the events and a letter from Romeo has been found.

PRINCE:
This letter doth make good the friar's words,
Their course of love, the tidings of her death:
And here he writes that he did buy a poison
Of a poor 'pothecary, and therewithal
Came to this vault to die, and lie with Juliet.
Where be these enemies? Capulet! Montague!
See, what a scourge is laid upon your hate,
That heaven finds means to kill your joys with love.
And I for winking at your discords too
Have lost a brace of kinsmen: all are punish'd.
CAPULET:
To brother Montague, give me thy hand:
This is my daughter's jointure, for no more
Can I demand.
MONTAGUE:
But I can give thee more:
For I will raise her statue in pure gold;
That while Verona by that name is known,
There shall no figure at such rate be set
As that of true and faithful Juliet.
CAPULET:
As rich shall Romeo's by his lady's lie;
Poor sacrifices of our enmity!
PRINCE:
A glooming peace this morning with it brings;
The sun, for sorrow, will not show his head:
Go hence, to have more talk of these sad things;
Some shall be pardon'd, and some punished:
For never was a story of more woe
Than this of Juliet and her Romeo.

Starting with this speech, explore how Shakespeare presents the theme of love.

Write about:
- how Shakespeare presents love in this extract
- how Shakespeare presents the theme of love in the play as a whole

[30 marks]
AO4 [4 marks]

THE PLAN

PARAGRAPH 1:

PARAGRAPH 2:

PARAGRAPH 3:

WRITING TIPS

EXAMPLE ESSAY STRUCTURE

There are many different ways to structure an essay. There is not one single way that works for every essay. Find a structure that you feel confident working with and adapt it to the question's needs. Below is a generic essay structure with some tips on what to include.

INTRODUCTION

Topic sentence using the wording of the question.

List of points you are going to make in the body of your essay.

MAIN BODY

Try to aim for 3-4 PEEL paragraphs.

If you are given an extract question try to divide your essay up equally, so half the essay is based on the extract and half is based on the play as a whole.

Make sure you spend time analysing your quotations fully. The best way to get great marks is to analyse quotes in-depth and provide alternative interpretations.

Don't forget to include context!

CONCLUSION

Link the points you have made in the body of your essay to the question.

Write a brief concluding thought on the question.

PEEL PARAGRAPH STRUCTURE

POINT

A short sentence at the beginning of your paragraph detailing the point you are about to make. Students often find it helpful to use the wording of the question in the point - though remember to relate it to the specific topic you are going to cover in your paragraph.

EVIDENCE

This is the quotation that you will use to support your point. It is best to keep the actual quote as short as possible - make sure you only include what you are going to break down and analyse.

EXPLAIN

Here you want to explain how your quotation relates to your point. Try to use close word analysis or literary technique analysis to uncover meaning in the text. You can also consider different interpretations and the effects of those interpretations. It is a good idea to include relevant context here. This should be the largest part of your paragraph.

LINK

Make sure you round off your point and clearly link it to the question. This is a good place to check you are actually answering the question fully.

EXAMPLE PARAGRAPH

HOW FAR DOES SHAKESPEARE PRESENT LORD CAPULET AS A GOOD FATHER?

POINT: Initially depicted as a caring father, concerned for his daughter's welfare in a patriarchal society, Lord Capulet ultimately reveals himself to be a product of his time.

EVIDENCE: We can see this in the quote, "[l]et two more summers wither in their pride ere we may think her ripe to be a bride."

EXPLAIN: The metaphor reveals the true nature of Lord Capulet's relationship with Juliet. He dehumanises and objectifies Juliet by comparing her to a fruit that is not 'ripe'. It demonstrates how Capulet views her as an object and commodity to be sold for the best price or, in this case, to the best man. Contextually, fathers in Elizabethan times had a duty to protect and improve their families' circumstances. One of the best ways to do this was by securing suitable and advantageous matches for their daughters. Paris, a nobleman and kinsman of the Prince, would be an excellent match for Juliet. So, on the one hand, Capulet could be viewed as a bad father as he rejects an advantageous match for Juliet, that would have secured her reputation, status, and financial situation. Alternatively, Lord Capulet can be viewed as an excellent father as he rejects Paris's generous offer out of his concern for Juliet's personal welfare. Furthermore, he demonstrates tactfulness as he does not reject the proposal outright but gently encourages Paris to wait 'two more summers'. The rhyming couplet reinforces Capulet's lighthearted tone.

LINK: Ultimately, Shakespeare constructs Lord Capulet as a complex multifaceted character who tries, and fails, to find balance for his young daughter in a strict, hierarchical, and patriarchal society.

GLOSSARY OF LITERARY TECHNIQUES

GLOSSARY OF LITERARY TECHNIQUES

ALLITERATION

The repetition of the same consonant sound, especially at the beginning of words.

ALLUSION

A reference to another event, person, place or work of literature. The allusion is usually implied rather than explicit and provides another layer of meaning to what is being said.

ANTAGONIST

A character that is the source of conflict in a literary work.

ASIDE

A dramatic device in which a character makes a short speech intended for the audience but not heard by the other characters on stage.

ASYNDETIC LISTING

When words are joined without the use of a conjunction, but with commas instead

COLLOQUIAL

Ordinary, everyday speech and language. Often very informal.

CONNOTATION

An implication or association attached to a word or phrase.

DIALOGUE

Direct speech between characters in a literary work.

DICTION

Another word for "vocabulary". The choice of words a writer uses.

GLOSSARY OF LITERARY TECHNIQUES

DRAMATIC IRONY

Where the audience's or reader's understanding of events or individuals in a work surpasses that of its characters.

END STOPPING

A verse line with a pause or stop at the end of it.

ENJAMBMENT

A line of verse that flows on into the next line without a pause (comma or full stop).

FIGURATIVE LANGUAGE

Language that is symbolic or metaphorical and not meant to be taken literally.

FORESHADOWING

A warning or indication of a future event.

GENRE

A particular type or style of writing — eg prose, poetry, tragedy, romance.

HYPERBOLE

Exaggerating for effect — it is not meant to be taken literally e.g. dying of boredom.

IMAGERY

The use of words to create a picture or "image" in the mind of the reader. Images can relate to any of the senses, not just sight.

INTERNAL RHYME

Rhyming words within a line rather than at the end of lines.

GLOSSARY OF LITERARY TECHNIQUES

IRONY

It occurs where a word or phrase has one surface meaning but another contradictory meaning is implied.

PLOT

The sequence of events in a poem, play, novel or short story that make up the main storyline.

PROTAGONIST

The main character or speaker in a text.

PUN

A play on words that have similar sounds but quite different meanings.

RULE OF THREE (TRICOLON)

Tricolon is a rhetorical term that consists of three parallel clauses, phrases, or words, which happen to come in quick succession without any interruption.

RHYME SCHEME

The pattern of rhymes in a poem.

RHYTHM

The 'movement' of the poem as created through the meter and the way that language is stressed within the poem.

SATIRE

The highlighting or exposing of human failings or foolishness through ridiculing them.

GLOSSARY OF LITERARY TECHNIQUES

SEMANTIC FIELD

A term used to describe a group of words, all of which share a similar concept, theme or subject.

SIMILE

A comparison using the words 'like' or 'as' to make the description more vivid.

SOLILOQUY

A dramatic device in which a character is alone and speaks his or her thoughts aloud.

STEROTYPE

Standardised, conventional ideas about characters, plots and settings.

STRUCTURE

The way a poem or play or other piece of writing has been put together.

SYMBOL

Symbols present things which represent something else. Often a material object representing something abstract.

SYNTAX

The way in which sentences are structured.

THEME

The central ideas that a writer explores through a text.

GLOSSARY OF LITERARY TECHNIQUES

METAPHOR

A comparison of one thing to another to make the description more vivid. The metaphor actually states that one thing is literally another.

MONOLOGUE

Monologue is an extended continuous speech, delivered in front of other characters and often has great thematic importance.

MOTIF

A recurring feature of a literary work that is related to the theme.

ONOMATOPOEIA

The use of words whose sounds copies the thing or process they describe, e.g. Boom.

OXYMORON

Phrase that consists of two words immediately next to one another that are contradictory: "living dead".

PARADOX

A statement that seems contradictory but may reveal a truth.

PERSONIFICATION

The attribution of human feelings, emotions, or sensations to an inanimate object.

INDEX OF QUOTES

INDEX OF QUOTES

INDEX OF QUOTES

TUTORING ENQUIRES

NEED A BIT MORE HELP?

Why not try **one-to-one** online tutoring tailored to your needs?

ABOUT THE TUTOR

Laura McQuiggin graduated with a 2:1 BA(Hons) degree in English Literature from Warwick University in 2020. She has worked extensively as a private tutor for over three years, taught over 2000 lessons, and received over 120 five-star reviews. She has an exemplary track record of helping students to achieve and supersede their academic goals.

For tutoring enquiries please contact via:
www.englishtuitiononline.co.uk

BOOK A FREE VIDEO MEETING TODAY!

Contact me via my website to arrange a free video meeting to discuss your child's needs.

SCAN ME

GET YOUR FIRST SESSION HALF PRICE!

Just quote '**JULIET 20**' in your email to have your first lesson for half price.

Printed in Great Britain
by Amazon

17600136R00052